D1408175

WE ♥ K-POP

ALL THE HOTTEST K-POP GROUPS!

Published in 2020 by Mortimer Children's Books

An Imprint of Welbeck Children's Limited, part of
Welbeck Publishing Group.

20 Mortimer Street London W1T 3JW

Text & design © Welbeck Children's Limited,
part of Welbeck Publishing Group.

Designed, written, and packaged by Dynamo Limited
Art editor: Deborah Vickers
Editor: Jenni Lazell
Picture research: Paul Langan

All rights reserved. No part of this publication may be reproduced,
 stored in a retrieval system, or transmitted in any form or by any
means, electronically, mechanical, photocopying, recording or
otherwise, without the prior permission of the copyright owners
and the publishers.

ISBN 978-1-83935-036-8

Printed in Dubai

10 9 8 7 6 5 4 3 2 1

CONTENTS

4 HELLO!

6 THE STORY SO FAR

10 TOP PICS: BTS

12 K-POP ESSENTIALS

14 TOP PICS: BLACKPINK

16 MEET THE BAND: BTS

18 TOP 10 MUSIC VIDEOS

20 TOP PICS: NCT

22 MEET THE BAND: BLACKPINK

24 REASONS WE LOVE K-POP

26 TOP PICS: TWICE

28 MEET THE BAND: TVXQ!

30 SIGNS YOU ARE A SUPERFAN

32 GALLERY: MEGA MOVERS

34 MEET THE BAND: NCT

36 TOP PICS: MONSTA X

38 MEET THE BAND: SUPER JUNIOR

40 AWARDS AND NOMINATIONS

42 K-POP BY NUMBERS

44 MEET THE BAND: TWICE

46 TOP PICS: RED VELVET

48 ICONIC DANCES

50 MEET THE BAND: MONSTA X

52 TOP PICS: SEVENTEEN

54 MEET THE BAND: RED VELVET

56 GALLERY: COLOR POP

58 MEET THE BAND: SEVENTEEN

60 TOP PICS: GIRLS' GENERATION

62 GALLERY: K-POP STYLE

64 MEET THE BAND: MAMAMOO

66 TOP PICS: EXO

68 MEET THE BAND: GIRLS' GENERATION

70 TOP COLLABS

72 MEET THE BAND: EXO

74 SOLO SUPERSTARS

76 FUTURE OF K-POP

78 K-POP QUIZ

80 PICTURE CREDITS

HELLO!

WELCOME TO YOUR ONE-STOP GUIDE TO ALL THINGS K-POP. THIS FAB FAN BOOK IS PACKED WITH PROFILES, FUN FACTS, AND AWESOME PICS!

Everyone is talking about K-Pop. The phenomenon has burst out of Korea and taken the world by storm. In the last 10 years, this genre of pop music has been able to find global fans for the first time. With its unforgettable melodies, awesome dancing, and iconic style, K-Pop really is the most fun ever.

In this book, you'll get to hang out with everyone from EXO to NCT and the infamous BTS. Don't know your Maknaes from your Sasaengs? Fear not—you'll have the chance to polish up your lingo with our essential K-Pop terms that everyone should know, too!

TURN THE PAGE TO START THE FUN . . .

THE STORY SO FAR

AFTER MORE THAN TWO DECADES, THE WORLD IS FINALLY READY TO EMBRACE K-POP. THIS IS HOW IT ALL HAPPENED...

YOU MAY ASSUME THAT K-POP IS A FAIRLY NEW GENRE OF MUSIC, BUT YOU'D BE WRONG. IT HAS TAKEN OVER 20 YEARS TO GET TO WHERE WE ARE TODAY!

Before finding worldwide audiences, K-Pop was a local phenomenon enjoyed in Korea. Today, people all over the world are hungry for the next K-Pop idol!

BTS storm the red carpet!

1995

SM Entertainment is founded by **Lee Soo-man**. Its artists include the likes of **TVQX!** and **EXO.**

LEE SOO-MAN

1996

H.O.T. (Highfive of Teenagers) are formed and sell over six million records in South Korea.

1997

Park Jin-young starts up JYP Entertainment—the agency responsible for **GOT7**, Rain, and many more.

K-Pop's first all-girl group, **S.E.S.**, sign with SM Entertainment.

THE FIRST WAVE

Let's kick things off with the first wave of K-Pop. Back in 1992, Seo Taiji and Boys performed their debut single, *I Know,* on a South Korean TV talent show. The hip-hop trio found fame overnight.

Seo Taiji and Boys were inspired by American hip-hop, heavy metal, and rock. They were like nothing else out there at the time!

RAIN went solo after Fanclub

> " K-Pop includes music videos, clothes, choreography, and social media. It is the total arts package. "
>
> **RAP MONSTER, BTS**

LET IT RAIN

In 1998, the boy group Fanclub debuted. Two years later they split but one of the members, Rain, went on to have a successful solo career.

Today, Rain is one of the most famous South Korean singer-songwriters, producers, and actors.

2000 →

Hallyu (Korean Wave) becomes recognized around the world. This was the first wave of South Korean music and culture.

In 2001, **MTV Korea** is launched, offering 24 hours of South Korean pop music.

2008 →

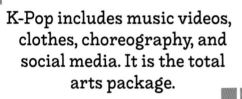

RAIN appear on the *Colbert Report* in the US. They become the first group to break into the American market.

2009 →

Girls' Generation release *Gee.* It becomes the first K-Pop song to reach 100 million views on YouTube in 2013.

GIRLS' GENERATION

FIRST IDOL GROUP

Five-piece H.O.T. (Highfive of Teenagers) catapulted onto the scene in 1996. These boys became K-Pop's first ever idol group.

> " We didn't mean to set the trend. We had no choice but to grow the market by ourselves and did what we did best. "
>
> **TONY AN, H.O.T.**

NEXT GENERATION

Next up came Girls' Generation. The group debuted in 2007 and made a big impression. They were the first group to perform on a US late night talk show when they appeared on the *Late Show with David Letterman*. Their iconic single, *Gee*, is now thought of as a K-Pop classic!

GIRLS' GENERATION

2012 →

The global obsession with K-Pop begins when **PSY's** *Gangnam Style* goes viral.

PSY

2013 →

PSY wins a Billboard Music Award for *Gangnam Style*. It is the most viewed video of the year, with over a billion hits!

2016 →

BLACKPINK become the fastest-selling K-Pop act. BTS are the first K-Pop group to top the Billboard Social 50 chart.

BLACKPINK

PASSING THE BATON

In 2017, Seo Taiji passed on the K-Pop baton to BTS while on stage in Seoul, and said: "This is your generation now." During their career, Seo Taiji and the Boys had changed censorship laws, which paved the way for future generations of South Korean stars.

BTS

GLOBAL SUCCESS

The BTS boys grabbed the mic and took K-Pop to the next level. They sold out stadium tours, scored a box office smash, broke records, and had awards coming out of their ears!

ESSENTIAL PLAYLIST

1. Gee – GIRLS' GENERATION
2. Sad Pain – SEO TAIJI
3. Free Way – RAIN
4. Candy – H.O.T.
5. Idol – BTS
6. Gangnam Style – PSY
7. Kill This Love – BLACKPINK
8. U – S.E.S.
9. Tell Me – WONDER GIRLS
10. Lucifer – SHINEE

2017 →

BTS win Top Social Artist at the Billboard Music Awards. Their *Love Yourself: Her* debuts in the Top 10 album charts all over the world.

2019 →

BLACKPINK'S hit single, *Kill This Love,* smashes YouTube records. They are the first girl group with a song to reach No.1 on iTunes in America since Destiny's Child in 2004.

BTS

2020 →

Global obsession level is reached. K-Pop now dominates global music charts and awards.

BTS raise the roof at the American Music Awards in Los Angeles on November 19, 2017.

> **Teamwork makes the dream work.**
>
> **RAP MONSTER, BTS**

K-POP ESSENTIALS

15 K-POP TERMS EVERY FAN SHOULD KNOW!

1

AEGYO
A group member's cute behavior. Jungkook from BTS has this mastered.

2

BIAS
B is for Bias, or your favorite member of your favorite K-Pop group.

3

COMEBACKS
K-Pop groups are famous for making yearly comebacks, usually with the release of multiple EPs or trilogies.

4

ENTERTAINMENT COMPANIES
JYP, YG, SM, Big Hit, and others are the record labels and management agencies that put K-Pop groups together, hire producers and songwriters, and operate every part of a K-Pop group's career.

5

FANDOMS
Every group has its fans, and each fandom has its own awesome name. BTS have their Army, Blackpink have their Blinks. What fandom do you belong to?

6

HALLYU
Also known as the "Korean Wave." Hallyu is a term used to describe the rising popularity of Korean culture.

7 HYUNG

A Korean word that means "older brother," used by a younger member to describe older members of a group.

8 IDOLS

An Idol is what you become when you successfully audition and become a member of a group.

9 MAKNAE

The term used to describe the youngest member of a group.

10 MVs

K-Pop is famous for MVs, or music videos. Featuring high production values and lots of outfit changes, they're a mesmerizing feast for the eyes. Check them out!

11 NUGUS

Idol groups that are relatively unpopular or unknown. But don't call anyone Nugu—it's rude!

12 ROOKIES
All new (under two years old) K-Pop groups. If your group finds success early, as NCT or Blackpink did, you become Monster Rookies!

13 SASAENGS

Obsessed fans who have no chill; they will do anything to get close to their favorite groups.

14 SUBUNITS
Many new groups, such as NCT, can be divided into subunits. Individual members within a group can be divided up to form separate smaller units.

15 TRAINEES

Wannabe idols who sign with an entertainment company and train, usually for several years, in the hope of becoming full-fledged idols.

BLACKPINK were the first K-Pop group to reach a billion views on YouTube with their single *Ddu-Du Ddu-Du.*

BTS

EVEN IF YOU'RE NOT A TOTAL K-POP SUPERFAN, YOU'VE PROBABLY HEARD OF BTS!

JIMIN
BIRTHDAY: October 13, 1995

FACT: Studied modern dance at high school

RM (RAP MONSTER)
BIRTHDAY: September 2, 1994

FACT: First member to join BTS

J-HOPE
BIRTHDAY: February 18, 1994

FACT: Once won a national dance competition

JUNGKOOK
BIRTHDAY: September 1, 1997

FACT: His dance to Billie Eilish's *bad guy* went viral

SUGA
BIRTHDAY: March 9, 1993

FACT: BTS' lead rapper

V
BIRTHDAY: December 30, 1995

FACT: His nickname "V" stands for Victory

JIN
BIRTHDAY: December 4, 1992

FACT: Oldest member of BTS

THE BOYS

This seven-piece supergroup are breaking records, smashing stereotypes, and lighting up the world. This talented bunch formed in 2013 and have been writing, producing, and dancing their way into our heart ever since.

> Breaking new records is important, but what I want most is to create performances and music that will satisfy our fans.

JUNGKOOK

THAT'S A RECORD!

Since they burst onto the scene, BTS have been paving the way for other K-Pop artists seeking a global fan base. From appearing on Ellen DeGeneres's show to featuring in *The Guinness Book of Records* (more than once!), BTS have made the world stop and listen to K-Pop. In 2017, they were the first K-Pop band to win a 2017 Billboard Music Award. Fast forward to 2019, and BTS were the first Korean Twitter account to reach 20 million followers.

 **ESSENTIAL PLAYLIST**

1. Boy With Luv
2. Blood Sweat & Tears
3. Mic Drop
4. Fake Love
5. DNA
6. Idol
7. Save Me
8. Dope
9. Spring Day
10. Fire

BTS STANDS FOR BANGTAN BOYS. THEY'RE AS FAMOUS FOR THEIR ICONIC DANCING AS THEY ARE FOR THEIR SONGS.

AWESOME ARMY

Their dedicated fanbase is known as the ARMY (Adorable Representative MC for Youth). BTS wouldn't be where they are today without the support of their loyal fans. The ARMY's social media activity has catapulted BTS into worldwide fame.

TOP 10 MUSIC VIDEOS

HERE ARE 10 K-POP MUSIC VIDEOS YOU NEED TO CHECK OUT! OUR FAVES SHOWCASE CREATIVE CHOREOGRAPHY, SLICK SETS, AND SERIOUS STORYTELLING SKILLS.

1
SONG: **FOLLOW**
BAND: **MONSTA X**

Everything about this video is fierce! From special effect snakes to their slick suits— we can't get enough of *Follow*.

2
SONG: **BOOM**
BAND: **NCT DREAM**

This comeback from NCT Dream broke away from their cute image, and created a more mature sound.

4
SONG: **DDU-DU DDU-DU**
BAND: **BLACKPINK**

This music video was the most viewed YouTube video by a K-Pop group in March 2020.

3
SONG: **FAKE LOVE**
BAND: **BTS**

This was their first smash hit to reach the US Top 10.

5

SONG: **FEAR**
BAND: **SEVENTEEN**

Tight melodies and spectacular special effects make Seventeen's *Fear* an out-of-this-world music video.

6

SONG: **CHEER UP**
BAND: **TWICE**

This beaut was the fastest K-Pop video to reach over 50 million views on YouTube.

7

SONG: **DNA**
BAND: **BTS**

This explosion of color is still their most viewed music video.

8

SONG: **ZIMZALABIM**
BAND: **RED VELVET**

The girls took the fantasy theme to the next level. We love the teacups, fireworks, and musical instruments playing all by themselves.

10

SONG: **OBSESSION**
BAND: **EXO**

Perfectly polished with a flawless dance routine, *Obsession* is all about good versus evil.

9

SONG: **HIP**
BAND: **MAMAMOO**

Get ready to be inspired by Mamamoo's empowering video. It's all about speaking up about what matters to you and being heard.

NCT appearing at Poptopia 2019, San Jose, California.

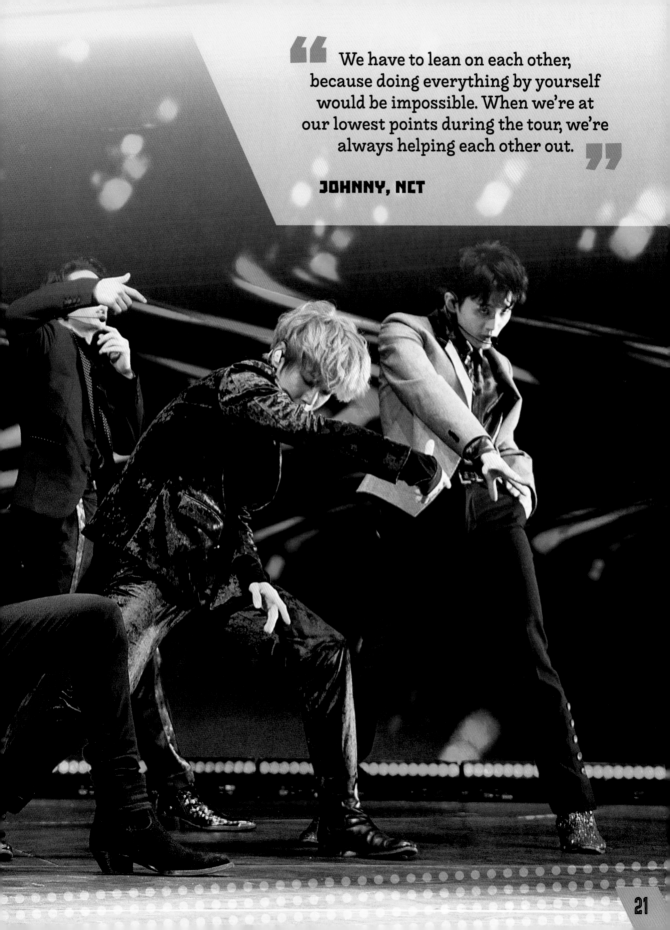

> **"** We have to lean on each other, because doing everything by yourself would be impossible. When we're at our lowest points during the tour, we're always helping each other out. **"**
>
> **JOHNNY, NCT**

BLACKPINK

FUSING UPTEMPO ELECTRO-POP WITH BOOMING HIP-HOP BEATS, THIS ALL-GIRL QUARTET HAS TAKEN THE K-POP WORLD BY STORM.

FANTASTIC FOUR

Jennie, Rosé, Lisa, and Jisoo began making music together in 2016, after being brought together as trainee idols by Seoul-based talent agency and record label YG Entertainment.

LISA

BIRTHDAY:
March 27, 1997

FACT: Sometimes called "Thailand Princess"

JISOO

BIRTHDAY:
January 3, 1995

FACT: Has a white belt in tae kwon do

JENNIE

BIRTHDAY:
January 16, 1996

FACT: Lived in New Zealand for five years

ROSÉ

BIRTHDAY:
February 11, 1997

FACT:
Nicknamed "Pasta"

INDEPENDENT WOMEN

Blackpink is the first K-Pop band to release both solo and group work at the same time. But loyal fans—known as Blinks or Blinkers—know that no matter how big the girls get on their own, they'll always come back together!

THE FUTURE IS BRIGHT

Blackpink's instant classics were brought together for the first time on the Japanese studio album, *In Your Area*, released in 2018. They found mega success in the same year with their collaboration on *Kiss and Make Up* with Dua Lipa. Their second album, *Kill This Love*, followed in 2019.

Blackpink were the first female K-Pop group to perform at Coachella Festival in California, and the first K-Pop group to rack up a billion views for music video *Ddu-Du Ddu-Du* on YouTube (take that, BTS!). The sky really is the limit for these four stars!

> " Our group name has a dual meaning: **BLACK** meaning strong and being confident, and **PINK** representing the feminine side of our group. "
>
> **JENNIE**

BLACKPINK
ESSENTIAL PLAYLIST

1. Whistle
2. Kiss and Make Up
3. Boombayah
4. Ddu-du Ddu-Du
5. Stay
6. As If It's Your Last
7. Forever Young
8. Really
9. Playing With Fire
10. See You Later

REASONS WE LOVE K-POP

JUST IN CASE YOU NEED ANY PERSUADING, HERE ARE A HANDFUL OF REASONS TO CELEBRATE THE WONDERS OF K-POP.

ARTISTIC

K-Pop groups are like a work of art. From slick choreography to amazing **special effects**, there is SO much more to this type of pop music than the ultra-famous *Gangnam Style*. There is a whole world of diverse acts to explore.

PROMOTING OPENNESS

K-Pop bands have created a platform for people to talk about their emotions. The genre has made it more acceptable for people to **open up** about their feelings.

SHOWSTOPPING

You don't need to dig very deep to discover that **live** K-Pop performances are like nothing else. These talented bands really are in a league of their own.

LEARN KOREAN

Want to learn Korean with **BTS**? Big Hit is bringing out an immersive language program to help you polish up your lingo.

STORYTELLING

Our favorite K-Pop songs and music videos flaunt some serious **storytelling** skills. Every song and music video will take you on a journey!

EMBRACING INDIVIDUALITY

They are not afraid to be themselves. From what they wear to how they behave, our fave K-Pop idols want to **stand out** from the crowd.

BREAKING LANGUAGE BARRIERS

It doesn't matter what language you speak, you will still have their **catchy** songs in your head.

IN SYNC

Despite celebrating each member's individuality, K-Pop groups know how to work together as a **unit**.

PUSHING BOUNDARIES

This genre is **ever-evolving** which keeps it fresh. Even when a K-Pop group finds fame and success, they keep experimenting and pushing for new ways to move and sound.

DEDICATION

It doesn't take a genius to figure out that successful K-Pop stars throw EVERYTHING into their life as idols. From being put through their paces as trainees, to the long hours of **rehearsals**.

TWICE perform on stage at 8th Gaon Chart K-Pop Awards in Seoul, South Korea, 2019.

> **"** We want to give people positive energy, and we also want to comfort people. **"**
>
> **NAYEON, TWICE**

TVXQ!

IT'S TIME TO HANG OUT WITH THE TVXQ! DUO. U-KNOW YUNHO AND MAX CHANGMIN WERE PART OF THE FIRST GENERATION OF K-POP STARS WHO SHAPED THE INDUSTRY.

INFLUENCERS

It's hard to imagine where K-Pop would be without TVXQ! As one of the first EVER K-Pop groups, this pair has influenced so many artists. When they first started out, K-Pop wasn't the global phenomenon that it is today.

TVXQ! MEANS "RISING GODS OF THE EAST" IN KOREAN.

U-KNOW YUNHO

BIRTHDAY: February 6, 1986

FACT: Released a mini album, *True Colors*

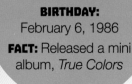

MAX CHANGMIN

BIRTHDAY: February 18, 1988

FACT: Has an IQ of 155!

WHEN 5 BECOME 2

Superfans will know that TVXQ! were once a five-piece group until Yoochun, Junso, and Jaejoong left. They have since formed their own K-Pop group called JYJ.

> " People cry, not because they are too weak. It's because they have been strong for too long. "
>
> **CHANGMIN**

10 YEARS LATER...

The boys were away from the stage for 10 years. They took the break due to military service, which is compulsory in Korea. As well as this, they also explored solo careers. Even after 10 years away, TVXQ! were welcomed back to a mix of old and new fans.

TVXQ!
ESSENTIAL PLAYLIST

1. Balloons
2. Catch Me
3. Android
4 Mirotic
5. Rising Sun
6. Purple Line
7. B.U.T
8. Spellbound
9. Lovin' You
10. Something

SIGNS YOU ARE A SUPERFAN

YOU KNOW NCT FROM BTS, AND BLACKPINK FROM RED VELVET, BUT HOW OBSESSED ARE YOU? HERE ARE EIGHT SIGNS THAT YOU'RE A TOTAL K-POP SUPERFAN!

1 ### YOU CAN . . .
name the members of ALL the biggest K-Pop groups. Easy. In fact, you probably know their birthdays by heart, too!

2 ### YOU SPEAK . . .
K-Pop. From Maknaes to Aegyos—you have completely mastered the K-Pop lingo.

3 ### K-POP AWARD SHOWS . . .
are the biggest events in your schedule. You always have the first scoop on who's nominated or won what. Well, you've got to show your support, right?

4 ### K-POP TRIVIA . . .
is your thing! When it comes to K-Pop history, you know your stuff. If there was a K-Pop quiz, it's your team we'd want to be on. No question!

5 ### YOU'VE GOT . . .
all the moves! Remember the routines for *Bubble Pop!* or *Sorry, Sorry?* Of course you do! K-Pop dance moves are life.

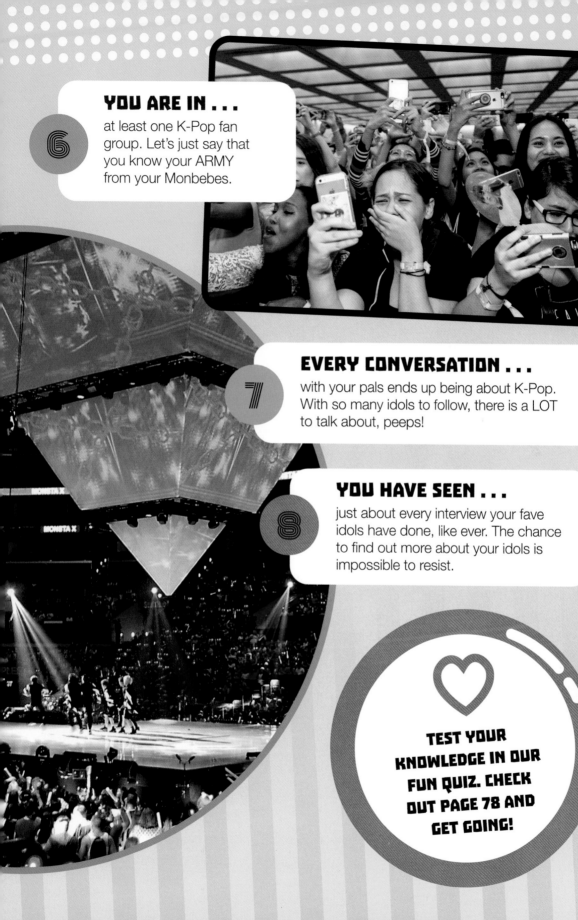

YOU ARE IN . . .

6

at least one K-Pop fan group. Let's just say that you know your ARMY from your Monbebes.

EVERY CONVERSATION . . .

7

with your pals ends up being about K-Pop. With so many idols to follow, there is a LOT to talk about, peeps!

YOU HAVE SEEN . . .

8

just about every interview your fave idols have done, like ever. The chance to find out more about your idols is impossible to resist.

TEST YOUR KNOWLEDGE IN OUR FUN QUIZ. CHECK OUT PAGE 78 AND GET GOING!

MEGA MOVERS

The K-Pop crew are as famous for their cool choreography as they are for their pop-tastic tunes. So, let's celebrate some big moments!

Hands up if you want to move like EXO!

MONSTA X flex their muscles! These boys put their all into every performance.

RED VELVET are in sync at the 8th Gaon Chart K-Pop Awards in 2019.

Check out TWICE'S super-cute signature move!

BLACKPINK pull off the hip thrust.

NCT 127 pull out some big moves in New York.

SEVENTEEN
soar into the air
with high-energy moves.

EXO show off their slick choreography.

The girls from TWICE know how to put on a show.

MONSTA X strut their stuff with a brush of the shoulder.

NCT

WITH A WHOPPING 21 MEMBERS IN TOTAL, IT'S NO WONDER THAT NCT HAVE CAPTURED EVERYONE'S ATTENTION!

TAG TEAM

NCT stands for "Neo Culture Technology" and is made up of four subunits. They act like a tag team, swapping in and out depending on what they're working on.

21 MEMBERS

4 SUBUNITS

SING IN 5 LANGUAGES

GLOBAL TAKEOVER

The ever-growing units that make up NCT are spread out all over the world. There are no limits to what this supergroup can do and how many of them there will be! Some members are top singers, others are incredible dancers or rappers. Combine all of these, and you have NCT.

Because there are so many members, I always feel supported.

DOYOUNG

SUBUNITS

With so many members to choose from, they can team up for the best combo for each track.

NCT U

NCT 127

NCT DREAM

WAYV

NCT ESSENTIAL PLAYLIST

1. Simon Says
2. Boss
3. Superhuman
4. Highway to Heaven
5. Limitless
6. Regular
7. Fire Truck
8. Switch
9. Chewing Gum
10. Without You

MONSTA X perform at the K-Pop World Festival in Seoul, South Korea, in 2017.

SUPER JUNIOR

FROM VIRAL DANCE CRAZES TO BREAKING INTO THE BILLBOARD CHARTS, SUJU ARE K-POP HEROES!

MIX IT UP

You don't have to be into a certain genre of music to appreciate Super Junior. This band releases everything from dance-pop to pop-rock, and electro-R&B with some ballads thrown in. Is there anything that these guys can't do?

> AS WELL AS SINGERS AND DANCERS, SOME OF SUJU'S MEMBERS ARE ACTORS, SONGWRITERS, AND MCs, TOO. SO MUCH TALENT FOR ONE BAND!

GOING STRONG

The iconic group, also known as SuJu, made a big comeback as a nine-piece band for their ninth album, *Timeless.* Say hello to **LEETEUK, HEECHUL, YESUNG, SHINDONG, EUNHYUK, SIWON, DONGHAE, RYEOWOOK,** and **KYUHYUN.** They've been making waves in the K-Pop world with SM Entertainment since 2005.

ELF ARMY

Super Junior have a super-cute name for their fans. **ELF** stands for "Everlasting Friends." Their army of followers have helped keep Super Junior at the top of their game for so long.

THEY'RE NOT SORRY SORRY

Super Junior have stood the test of time and have managed to stay popular since 2005. Over the years, some of the members have changed, but they've never lost their distinctive band identity. They've stayed true to themselves and their adoring fans.

> We want to continue to grow as a group, so that when the public thinks "K-Pop," Super Junior becomes a household name . . .

LEETEUK

SUPER JUNIOR
ESSENTIAL PLAYLIST

1. Sorry Sorry
2. Bittersweet
3. Mr. Simple
4. It's You
5. SUPER Clap
6. Miracle
7. Black Suit
8. No Other
9. I Think I
10. One More Time

AWARDS AND NOMINATIONS

WE ALL KNOW THAT K-POP IS WELL ON ITS WAY TO WORLD DOMINATION. HERE ARE SOME STANDOUT MOMENTS WHEN OUR FAVE IDOLS TOTALLY OWNED THE AWARDS!

MNET ASIAN MUSIC AWARDS (MAMA) 2019

- ★ **BTS** scooped up Artist of the Year
- ★ **BTS** won 4 Daesang
- ★ **TWICE** nabbed Best Female Group and Best Dance Performance (Female Group)
- ★ World Performer was won by **MONSTA X**
- ★ **ITZY** won Best New Female Artist

GOLDEN DISC AWARDS 2020

- ★ **BTS** grabbed TikTok Golden Disc Popularity, plus the Fan's Choice K-Pop Star Award
- ★ **MAMAMOO** were awarded Best Group
- ★ Rookie Artist of the Year went to **ITZY** and **TXT**

SEOUL MUSIC AWARDS 2020

- ★ **TAEYEON** (from **GIRLS' GENERATION**) won the grand prize for digital music with her single, *Four Seasons*, released in May, 2019
- ★ **BTS** won the grand prize for the third time running for their iconic *Map of the Soul: Persona*

ITUNES

BLACKPINK'S *Kill This Love* was the first iTunes No. 1 by an Asian girl group.

YOUTUBE BILLION VIEWS CLUB

★ **BLACKPINK'S** music video *Ddu-Du Ddu-Du* racked up over a billion views on YouTube. This made them the first K-Pop group to achieve this.

★ They actually broke another YouTube record with *Kill This Love*. In just two days, it was watched over a million times.

TIKTOK

The fastest time to reach 1 million followers on TikTok goes to **BTS.** After announcing they were joining, it took just 3 hours and 31 minutes for their ARMY to spread the word!

BILLBOARD 200

★ **BTS** are THE record-breaking band. They recorded the first K-Pop album to spend a whole year on the Billboard 200 with their album, *Love Yourself: Answer*. The same album made BTS the first Korean act to earn an RIAA Platinum Album Certification.

ASIAN ARTIST AWARDS

★ Seven-member boy group **GOT7** won their first Daesang in 2019 with two comebacks— *Spinning Top : Between Security & Insecurity* and *Call My Name*.

DREAM DEBUT

ITZY broke the record for fastest K-Pop debut music video to gain 100 million views with *DALLA DALLA*.

K-POP BY NUMBERS

WE'VE CRUNCHED SOME NUMBERS, SO THAT YOU DON'T HAVE TO!

1992

♪ THE YEAR THAT **K-POP** WAS BORN

4 K-POP ALBUMS

HAVE MADE IT TO **NUMBER 1** ON THE BILLBOARD 200

2 K-POP ACTS

HIT **NUMBER 1** IN THE BILLBOARD 200 CHARTS—**SuperM** AND **BTS**

163 WEEKS

BTS SPENT 163 WEEKS AT **NUMBER 1** ON THE BILLBOARD SOCIAL 50

20 RECORDS

BROKEN BY **BTS** (SO FAR!)

21 MEMBERS IN **NCT**—THE BIGGEST K-POP GROUP AROUND RN!

BLACKPINK'S *KILL THIS LOVE* MV

FASTEST VIDEO TO REACH **100 MILLION** YOUTUBE VIEWS

34 MILLION

34 MILLION SUBSCRIBERS FOR **BLACKPINK'S** YOUTUBE CHANNEL

 **20.31 MINS**

MUSIC VIDEO *LOVEY-DOVEY* BY **T-ARA**

2009

SUPER JUNIOR SHOOK UP K-POP WITH THEIR VIRAL SONG AND MV *SORRY SORRY*

3 **GUINNESS WORLD RECORDS** FOR **BTS'S** *BOY WITH LUV* MUSIC VIDEO

 The number of hours it took **BTS** to reach 3 million followers on TikTok

LO SIENTO BY **SUPER JUNIOR** WAS THE FIRST K-POP SONG TO REACH THE LATIN BILLBOARD CHART. IT REACHED **NUMBER 13.**

*Stats correct at the time of writing.

TWICE

SINCE DEBUTING WITH *CHEER UP* IN 2015, TWICE HAVE BECOME K-POP'S BIGGEST ALL-GIRL GROUP! HERE'S WHY WE LOVE THEM ...

♬ THEIR CATCHY SINGLE *CHEER UP* WAS SOUTH KOREA'S MOST DOWNLOADED SONG OF THE YEAR.

MEET THE TEAM

♥ JIHYO

♥ MINA

♥ CHAEYOUNG

♥ DAHYUN

♥ MOMO

♥ NAYEON

♥ SANA

♥ JEONGYEON

♥ TZUYU

REALITY TV

JYP entertainment put Twice together through a reality TV show called *Sixteen* in 2015. Why are they called Twice? It's because of the way that they win everyone over with their look and sound! Double whammy.

COLOR POP

Twice are all about having fun and being positive. Each member has her own unique personality and style! Their energetic and fun sound is a clever mix of hip-hop, rap, jazz, and electronica. Twice describe their genre as "color pop."

 I believe our team is overflowing with energy when we're on stage . . . I think it's all possible due to us getting along and our teamwork being so great. "

JIHYO

TWICE
ESSENTIAL PLAYLIST

1. Candy Pop
2. Dance the Night Away
3. Heart Shaker
4. Knock Knock
5. Cheer Up
6. Yes or Yes
7. Likey
8. Wow
9. Merry and Happy
10. TT

ON THE ROAD

The year 2019 was a big one for Twice! They toured the United States for the first time, including three arena dates. They also played in Japan, where some of the biggest venues sold out.

RED VELVET perform at KCON 2015—the annual K-Pop convention held in Los Angeles.

> **"** We want to be a group who encourages people, and hope they can learn how to love and be themselves, living the life they were meant to. **"**
>
> **JOY, RED VELVET**

ICONIC DANCES

GET INTO THE GROOVE WITH THESE INCREDIBLE DANCE MOVES!

BODY ROLLING

If you're going to learn just one K-Pop move, it should be the body roll. Simply roll your body slowly from head to toe like a ripple. For the perfect technique, watch BTS's Jimin.

HIP-HOP

Urban dance moves make up a lot of K-Pop routines. It's all about the swagger. The more body popping, the better! This edgy choreography was inspired by breakdancing from back in the 80s and 90s, which came over to Korea from America.

ACROBATICS

No K-Pop performance is complete without some high-energy acrobatics! Some of the finest performers fuse martial arts with gymnastics. Blackpink's Lisa and Rosé are complete pros when it comes to flawless and gravity-defying moves.

THE ARROGANT DANCE

This dance move was made famous by Brown Eyed Girls. It's all about swaying your hips from side to side. For the best results, you should cross your arms and try to look like you really don't care! Go on, take a spin . . .

BAR BAR BAR

This dance is from the MV for 2013's chart-topping hit, *Bar Bar Bar*. You'll need a few friends for this to work. Stand in a row, and take turns ducking down at alternate times. As the person next to you ducks down, you stand up, and vice versa.

No matter what moves you're trying, being in sync is key. It's all down to timing and being in tune with the rest of your band. The only way to nail this is to practice and then, practice some more…

MONSTA X

LET'S HANG OUT WITH MONSTA X AND FIND OUT WHAT THEY'RE ALL ABOUT!
WE GUARANTEE YOU'LL BE A MEMBER OF THEIR MONBEBES IN NO TIME . . .

ALL ABOARD

The all-boy group was put together by Starship Entertainment. Monsta X debuted on a TV show called *No Mercy!* in 2015. Since then, they've racked up millions of YouTube views and followers!

KIHYUN
BIRTHDAY:
November 22, 1993
FACT: Can play piano and guitar

MINHYUK
BIRTHDAY:
November 3, 1993
FACT: Joker of the group

I.M.
BIRTHDAY:
January 26, 1996
FACT: Favorite place to be is Osaka, Japan

WONHO
BIRTHDAY:
March 1, 1993
FACT: Lead vocalist and lead dancer

SHOWNU
BIRTHDAY:
June 18, 1992
FACT: Started as a trainee with K-Pop group GOT7

HYUNGWON
BIRTHDAY:
January 15, 1994
FACT: Sleeps the most in the group

JOOHONEY
BIRTHDAY:
January 16, 1996
FACT: Lived in New Zealand for five years

DOUBLE MEANING

The name Monsta X has two meanings. It means "my star" or "monsters conquering the K-Pop scene." The "X" stands for an unknown existence.

MONSTA X
ESSENTIAL PLAYLIST

1. Follow
2. X
3. Stuck
4. Rush
5. Perfect Girl
6. Someone's Someone
7. Who Do U Love?
8. Alligators
9. Jealousy
10. Beautiful

SUPER CUTE

They call their fans Monbebes. But do you know why? In French, "mon" means "my" and "bébé" means "baby."

> " Our fans are everything to us. They see us perform, they see us grow. The reason we are performing every day is them and only them. "
>
> **I.M.**

SEVENTEEN nail their ambitious performance at the 8th Gaon Chart K-Pop Awards, 2019.

> If you watch our performances you can see that we constantly use the number of members on our team to our advantage. It's our strength. We can harness and channel so much energy, and that power is something we can relay to directly to our audience.
>
> **YOONA, SEVENTEEN**

RED VELVET

THIS ALL-GIRL GROUP HAVE BEEN ON THE SCENE SINCE 2014 WHEN THEY RELEASED THEIR SINGLE, *HAPPINESS*. THE BAND WASN'T QUITE COMPLETE UNTIL YERI WAS ADDED TO THE MIX A YEAR LATER!

SEULGI

BIRTHDAY: February 10, 1994

FACT: Red Velvet's main dancer

JOY

BIRTHDAY: September 3, 1996

FACT: Starred in TV dramas

YERI

BIRTHDAY: March 5, 1999

FACT: Last to join the group in 2015

IRENE

BIRTHDAY: March 29, 1991

FACT: Nickname is "Baechu," which means "cabbage"

WENDY

BIRTHDAY: February 21, 1994

FACT: Plays the flute, piano, saxophone, and guitar

FLASHBACK!

Did you know that before Red Velvet, Irene, Wendy Seulgi, and Yeri were in SM Rookies—a team of SM Entertainment's trainees.

TROPHY TIME

As well as a growing fan base, Red Velvet also have a growing trophy collection! From the 2015 Golden Disc New Artist Award to the Best Female Group in 2017 Mnet Asian Music Award.

> **"** We want to tell our fans that you can be whoever you want, as long as you have confidence. **"**
>
> **WENDY**

TROLLS ON TOUR

Red Velvet joined the cast of *Trolls* for the *Troll World Tour* movie in 2020. The star-studded cast included Anna Kendrick and Justin Timberlake.

RED VELVET
ESSENTIAL PLAYLIST

1. Ice Cream Cake
2. Peek-A-Boo
3. Red Flavor
4. Happiness
5. Sunny Side Up
6. Bad Boy
7. Look
8. Kingdom Come
9. Butterflies
10. Dumb Dumb

COLOR POP

Idols don't shy away from bold colors —hair and clothes included! So let this gallery brighten up your day.

Rainbow color palette.

Perfect pastel-blue hues!

Livening things up with an array of jazzy jackets.

Orange hair and clashing colors from NCT.

Lush lilac locks.

Busy prints teamed with bold block tights!

Looking fly in emerald shirts and bow ties.

Vibrant red all the way.

Sequins and neon? What's not to love!

Pink, pink, and more pink with Momoland.

SEVENTEEN

IF YOU DON'T KNOW ABOUT SEVENTEEN, WHERE HAVE YOU BEEN? HERE'S ALL YOU NEED TO KNOW TO BE A CARAT, FROM FAN CLUBS TO MASCOTS AND HOW THE BAND FOUND THEIR NAME.

WHO ARE THEY?

This 13-member group were put together by Pledis Entertainment in 2015. They're called Seventeen because it was the average age of the group when they debuted. Plus, it has 13 members + 3 subunits + 1 group.

♡ DK   ♡ WOOZI
♡ THE8
♡ JEONGHAN   ♡ DINO
♡ VERNON
♡ HOSHI   ♡ MINGYU
♡ S.COUPS
♡ JOSHUA   ♡ JUN
♡ SEUNGKWAN
♡ WONWOO

17 CARAT

Seventeen's fan club is called Carat. They took the name from the title of Seventeen's first album, *17 CARAT*. These boys gave their fans plenty to love with their reality show called *Seventeen TV*. It was all about the band before they debuted.

> These are the stories we want to tell, and we're making it ourselves, rather than just putting on something made for us. It feels more profound.
>
> **WOOZI**

MEGA MASCOT

The group have their very own mascot. It's true! Member Mingyu created the doll named BongBong. The idols take their mascot with them to shows and on tour!

SEVENTEEN
ESSENTIAL PLAYLIST

1. Fear
2. Call Call Call!
3. Good To Me
4. Mansae
5. Getting Closer
6. Let Me Hear You Say
7. Hit
8. Very Nice
9. Clap
10. Don't Wanna Cry

GIRLS' GENERATION have released an impressive nine studio albums and 28 singles.

K-POP STYLE

Here is a selection of our favorite
K-Pop styles. Which do YOU like best?

EXID flaunt their individual and quirky styles.

We're loving 2NE1's retro 80s inspired look.

EXO embrace their sporty side all in black and white.

Striped tees and jeans for a relaxed but trendy style.

MONSTA X are a vision of pastel-pink suits.

It's back to school for EXO with matching blazers and ties.

MONSTA X make a statement dressed head to toe in black.

We love this tangerine tailored look for GFRIEND!

(G)I-DLE go urban with cool prints and high-waisted pants.

MAMAMOO

SINCE DEBUTING IN 2014 WITH THEIR SINGLE, *MR. AMBIGUOUS*, MAMAMOO HAVE RELEASED ONE HIT AFTER ANOTHER.

WHEEIN
BIRTHDAY:
April 17, 1995
FACT: Calls herself "the snack queen"

SOLAR
BIRTHDAY:
February 21, 1991
FACT: The mom of the group

MOONBYUL
BIRTHDAY:
December 22, 1992
FACT: Created the choreography for *Mr. Ambiguous*

HWASA
BIRTHDAY:
July 23, 1995
FACT: Loves to cook for the group

THEIR JOURNEY TO SUCCESS

This South Korean all-girl group was formed by RBW. Even their debut went down in history as one of the best. Since bursting onto the K-Pop scene, the group have released three full-length albums: *Melting*, *Reality in Black,* and *4colors*.

K-POP QUEENS

Mamamoo won *Queendom*, which is a talent contest (a little like *The X-Factor*). Acts compete each week in a battle to win the title. They must then get voted in by the audience as well as earning points.

MAMAMOO
ESSENTIAL PLAYLIST

1. You're the Best
2. Yes I am
3. Starry Night
4. Woo Hoo
5. Peppermint Chocolate
6. Mr. Ambiguous
7. Girl Crush
8. New York
9. Piano Man
10. HIP

> We want to show other sides of ourselves rather than just a bright and happy image, but there aren't many chances to do that, so it's too bad.

MAMAMOO

SMASHED IT

Their single, *HIP*, made Mamamoo the fourth female act to top the World Albums and World Digital Song Sales. This was their first number 1 on the World Digital Songs Chart!

Here's a flashback to 2013, when EXO made a big impression performing on the Mnet M Countdown show in South Korea.

> "I'd like to make everything that I do enjoyable for everyone. When I'm enjoying myself, I make sure that not only I find joy in the process, but to also strive for a positive outcome at the very end."
>
> **CHANYEOL, EXO**

GIRLS' GENERATION

IF YOU LOVE K-POP, YOU'LL KNOW WHO GIRLS' GENERATION ARE! THEY'VE BEEN AT THE TOP OF THEIR GAME EVER SINCE THEIR SMASH HIT, *GEE*.

THE GIRLS, WHO ARE SOMETIMES KNOWN AS SNSD, HAVE INSPIRED A GENERATION OF NEW K-POP ACTS.

♥ SOOYOUNG

♥ SUNNY

♥ CHAEYOUNG

MEET THE GROUP

The nine idols were put together by SM Entertainment, and they've been breaking records and topping charts ever since! South Korea even nicknamed them the "Nation's Girl Group."

♥ HYOYEON

♥ YURI

♥ YOONA

♥ TIFFANY

♥ SEOHYUN

♥ NAYEON

MUSICAL MILESTONE

To celebrate 10 years together, Girls' Generation made a special album, *Holiday Night*. This was back in 2017, and it topped the Billboard World Album charts.

> ## SO, WHAT'S THE SECRET TO STAYING BIG FOR OVER A DECADE?
>
> "We were able to reach 10 years together because we were brave and strong every step of the way ... "

TAEYEON

GIRLS' GENERATION
ESSENTIAL PLAYLIST

1. Girls
2. Holiday
3. Mr. Mr.
4. I Got A Boy
5. Hoot
6. Gee
7. Paparazzi
8. All Night
9. Girls' Generation
10. Tell Me Your Wish

BEHIND THEIR NAME

Fans mostly call the group SNSD, but do you know why? Well, it comes from their Korean name, which is So Nyeo Shi Dae.

TOP COLLABS

HOW MANY OF THESE COOL COLLABS HAVE YOU HEARD OF? HERE ARE SOME OF THE BEST TIMES K-POP CREWS TEAMED UP ON TRACKS.

BTS + LIL NAS X

Hip-hop and country star **LIL NAS X** collaborated with **BTS** on a remix of his hit, *Old Town Road*. Their version was called *Seoul Town Road*. Together they created a whole new genre of music—K-country-pop. BTS's first ever Grammy appearance happened as a result of this track!

NICKI MINAJ + BTS

Have you heard the **BTS** and **NICKI MINAJ** remix of *Idol*? If you haven't, then you're in for a treat! *Idol* was an awesome color explosion to start with, but adding Nicki into the mix was the cherry on the cake.

BLACKPINK + DUA LIPA

What happens when some of your favorite artists work together? The *Kiss and Make Up* Dua Lipa track, that's what! Dua is famous for her hits including *New Rules* and *Don't Start Now*. They even performed together at Coachella in 2019.

JASON DERULO + NCT 127

Let's Shut Up & Dance was the hit that came out of the collab between Jason Derulo, Lay Zhang from EXO, and NCT 127. Packed with cool choreography, the music video is a celebration of how music brings people together from around the globe!

RED VELVET + ELLIE GOULDING + DIPLO

We all remember Ellie Goulding's *Close To Me*, right? Well, Ellie asked Red Velvet to get involved on a remix of the track with Diplo. As you'd expect, the results were awesome. Go listen now—if you haven't already!

EXO

THIS ULTRA-TALENTED GROUP IS ONE TO WATCH! EXO SURE HAVE MADE THEIR MARK.

EXO IS SECOND ONLY TO BTS WITH THEIR NUMBER OF CHARTING ALBUMS ON THE BILLBOARD 200.

WHO'S IN THE BAND

▷ XIUMIN

▷ LAY

▷ SUHO

▷ CHEN

▷ BAEKHYUN

▷ CHANYEOL

▷ D.O

▷ KAI

▷ SEHUN

SOARING TO SUCCESS

The band was formed by SM Entertainment in 2011 and debuted in 2012. Exo have skyrocketed to success ever since! They even made it into the 2018 *Guinness Book of World Records* for winning the most Daesangs (Grand Prizes) at Mnet Asian Music Awards.

JOIN FORCES

Exo came into being when the two subunits called Exo-K and Exo-M merged together. The band releases music in three different languages—Korean, Mandarin, and Japanese.

WINTER OLYMPICS

These boys were lucky enough to perform at the 2018 Winter Olympics in Seoul. Their show was nothing short of spectacular, with fireworks galore. Many believe that they were asked to perform because they have become a symbol of unity.

 **ESSENTIAL PLAYLIST**

1. Moonlight
2. Stronger
3. Growl
4. Love Shot
5. Baby Don't Cry
6. Mama
7. Monster
8. Lucky One
9. Unfair
10. What is Love

> " The relationship between the members, the teamwork we have, that's very important. "
>
> **SUHO**

SOLO SUPERSTARS

THE K-POP WORLD ISN'T ALL ABOUT BANDS AND TROOPS OF PERFORMERS. THERE ARE LOTS OF AWESOME SOLO ACTS, TOO.

RAIN

Long before a lot of the world had even heard of K-Pop, **RAIN** was tirelessly auditioning and rehearsing to pursue his dream of stardom. Way back in 2007, *Time* magazine named Rain as one of the "100 People Who Shape Our World." He went on to tour the world and released 7 albums and 28 singles.

SUNMI

SUNMI started out as part of South Korean girl group Wonder Girls, before going solo in 2017. She's now at the top of her game! Sumni's bold tracks are all about drama and witty wordplay, and we can't get enough of it. Her single, *Lalalay*, was viewed over 5 million times in its first week!

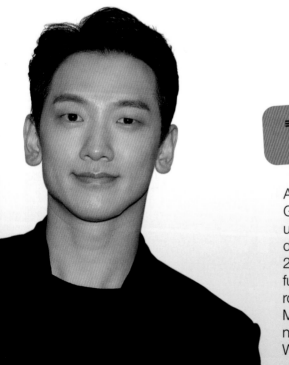

TAEYEON

After leaving Girls' Generation, the uber-talented **TAEYEON** debuted as a soloist in 2015. Her sound is a fusion of R&B, pop, and rock. Her first album—My Voice—went in at number 2 on Billboard's World Albums chart.

BoA is the influential K-Pop solo act dubbed "the Queen of Korean Pop." Since being discovered by SM Entertainment, BoA has gone on to sell millions of records around the world. She speaks Korean, Japanese, and English, and has recorded songs in Chinese, too! Listen to her debut solo album, *My Heart,* if you haven't already.

This idol has totally earned her place as one of Korea's biggest K-Pop acts this decade. Her vocal range is exceptional, and her indie sound has made her stand out from other acts of the K-Pop genre. **IU** has also written lots of her top tracks, including most of her album, *Palette*.

This unstoppable K-pop idol has been in training since he was just 12 years old. Fast forward to now, and **TAEMIN** is still just as energetic, plus he has a string of hits to his name. *Drip Drop* and *Move* are some of our favorites, but see what you think . . .

THE FUTURE OF K-POP

WITH MORE ACTS MAKING THEIR MARK ON THE K-POP SCENE, THERE'S LOTS TO LOOK FORWARD TO. WHICH ACTS (OLD AND NEW!) ARE YOU EXCITED ABOUT? HERE ARE OUR TOP PICKS . . .

(G)I-DLE

There's no risk of ever getting bored with girl group **(G)I-DLE.** Together, Miyeon, Minnie, Soojin, Soyeon, Yuqi, and Shuhua have gripped everyone's attention with their high-concept hits. Get a taster of what they're about by checking out *Lion* and *Uh-Oh*. You won't be disappointed!

ITZY

Girl group **ITZY** picked up a MAMA for Best New Female Artist 2019. The girls are named Yeji, Lia, Ryujin, Chaeryeong, and Yuna. Their hit *DALLA DALLA* became the fastest K-Pop debut music video to reach 100 million views. We can't wait to see what the future has in store for this unstoppable force of five.

MONSTA X

We predict tons of exciting stuff to come from **MONSTA X.** They have a big tour on the horizon, for a start! Seeing as they have a super-successful arena tour, we're not surprised one bit that they are continuing to ride that wave.

Lighting up the stage is the fierce six-member group called **EVERGLOW.** Their debut single, *Bon Bon Chocolat,* was enough to win us over! We just hope they don't keep us waiting too long before feeding us more hits!

EVERGLOW

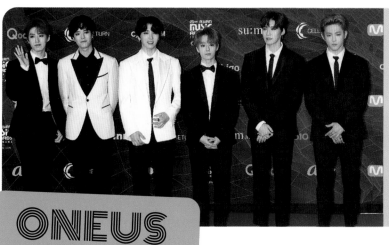

ONEUS

This boy band is on the same label as Mamamoo. So if they're even half as good, then we're in for a treat. Their song *Lit* takes its inspiration from traditional Korean culture, fusing it with hip-hop and trap for a fresh sound. We're sure these guys are going to shine on the scene.

BLACKPINK'S *Kill This Love* was the first single by an Asian girl group to reach number 1 in the US iTunes store. With American tours and multilingual tracks, they're sure to pick up even more of a following. These gals may just be the next BTS when it comes to global success!

BLACKPINK

K-POP QUIZ

SO YOU THINK YOU KNOW ALL THERE IS TO KNOW ABOUT THE K-POP UNIVERSE? TAKE THE ULTIMATE K-POP QUIZ.

1 Which 13-member K-Pop group has a mascot named BongBong?

2 Name Monsta X's fan group.

3 What was the name of Red Velvet's first single?

4 How many members are part of NCT in total?

5 Who has fans called Blinks?

6 Red Velvet joined the cast for which movie?

7 Name the band who released the viral music video, *Sorry Sorry*.

8 Which girl group released a debut single called *Happiness*?

9 What is the name of BTS's fanbase?

10 Which band won Best Group at the Golden Disc Awards 2020?

11 Name the Blackpink track that got the band into YouTube's Billion Views Club.

12 How many Guinness World Records did BTS's *Boy With Luv* music video get?

13 Which band debuted on a show called *No Mercy!* in 2015?

14 SNSD is the shortened name for which girl group?

15 At which sporting event did EXO perform in 2018?

ANSWERS: Seventeen, 2. Monbebe, 3. Happiness, 4. 21, 5. Blackpink, 6. Trolls World Tour, 7. Super Junior, 8. Red Velvet, 9. ARMY, 10. Mamamoo, 111. Ddu-Du Ddu-Du, 12. 3, 13. Monsta X, 14. Girls' Generation, 15. Winter Olympics in Seoul.

Picture credits

The publishers would like to thank the following sources for their kind permission to reproduce the pictures in this book. Every effort has been made to acknowledge correctly and contact the source and/or copyright holder of each picture any unintentional errors or omissions will be corrected in future editions of this book.
Key: T=top, B=bottom, L=left, R=right, C=center.

ALAMY: /Newscom: 6B; Yonhap/Newscom: 28L, 28BL
GETTY IMAGES: /Imeh Akpanudosen: 8BL; /Neilson Barnard: 9; /Bryan Bedder: 33TR; /Michael Boardman: 63BR; /Daniel Boczarski/Redferns: 62BL; /Choi Soo-Young/Multi-Bits: 63T; /The Chosunilbo JNS/Multi-Bits: 7B, 8L, 19BR, 49R, 60-61, 69, 74R; /Chung Sung-Jun: 18BR, 19TR, 26-27, 33TL, 33R, 48TR, 52-53, 54, 58, 63BL, 76R, 77BR; /Dia Dipasupil: 71TR; /Greg Doherty: 31TR; /Jim Dyson/Redferns: 70BR; /Rich Fury: 18L, 51L, 51BR, 63L, 71TL; /Steve Granitz/WireImage: 6T, 56R; /Han Myung-Gu/WireImage: 22, 32BL, 49TL, 62R, 66-67, 74BL, 74BR, 75L; /ilgan Sports/Multi-Bits: 48-49, 49L, 72, 73B; /Ken Ishii: 62L; /Steve Jennings/WireImage: 71R; /Scott Kowalchyk/CBS: 23, 32-33; /John Lamparski: 50; /Jamie McCarthy: 34-35; /Maddie Meyer: 73T; /Ethan Miller: 71BR; /JC Olivera: 43, 80; /Terence Patrick/CBS: 14-15; /Jun Sato/WireImage: 77L; /John Shearer: 4-5, 24-25; /Matthew Simmons: 30-31, 46-47, 71BL; /Starnews/AFP: 57L; /TPG: 56C; /Ten Asia/Multi-Bits: 75BR; /Michael Tran/FilmMagic: 33BR; /Unioncom/Visual China Group: 8-9, 39B; /Visual China Group: 7T, 12, 32L, 33BL, 62-63, 68, 76BL; /Kevin Winter: 17, 42; /Sam Yeh/AFP: 39T; /Paul Zimmerman: 25T
PA IMAGES: /TPG/Zuma Press: 65; /Young Ho/SIPA USA: 36-37, 40-41, 45B, 57R
SHUTTERSTOCK: /Aflo: 55, 56B; /Ondrej Deml: 71BC; /EPA: 29; /imageSPACE: 20-21, 35B, 56-57T; /Imagine China: 32BR, 59; /Kim Hee-Chul/EPA: 8BR, 32R, 41, 45T, 62BR; /Lee Jin-Man/AP: 56L; /Seokyong Lee/Penta Press: 35TL, 57B; /Frank Micelotta: 10-11, 19L; /Matt Sayles/Invision/AP: 70C; /Startraks: 57T; /Terence Tan/AP: 38; /Debby Wong: 71L; /Yonhap/EPA-EFE: 16, 44, 48L, 56-57B, 64, 75TR, 76L, 77T, 78-79